PRESENTS

THE DEFINITIVE GUIDE TO
FORTNITE
2026

A TOTALLY INDEPENDENT PUBLICATION

ISBN 978-1-917522-13-7

Images © Epic Games.

A Pillar Box Red Publication

Written by Naomi Berry
Designed by Adam Wilsher

READY UP!

When it comes to games that completely dominate the cultural conversation, Fortnite is basically in a league of its own. Since Epic Games dropped this masterpiece back in 2017, the phenomenon has only grown more massive and lightning-fast, basically writing the playbook for what live service gaming should look like. With somewhere between 2-4 million players jumping in daily, it's safe to say we're all part of something pretty big here.

This guide is your all-access pass to Fortnite mastery - packed with the game's epic history, the evolution of those iconic islands, breakdowns of every game mode, plus survival tactics and weapon guides that'll have you dominating in no time. We've also thrown in some quizzes to help you discover your perfect play style and test just how much you really know, along with puzzles to keep your brain warm between matches.

So board the battle bus with this guide by your side - we're about to tear through the island and everything it throws at us. Time to construct, clash, and outlast every last opponent out there. Next stop: Victory Royale!

CONTENTS

GLOSSARY

Fortnite is creeping ever-closer to its 10 year anniversary, but it's still fair to say that the game is far from finished. With constant updates, collabs, new game modes, and wild events dropping all the time, the Fortnite universe keeps expanding faster than a rift in the sky. And with all that new stuff comes a whole new wave of lingo to keep up with.

Whether you're totally cracked or just dropping in for the first time, there's a lot of Fortnite-speak flying around: in matches, in chats, and all over the expanded Fortnite universe (hey, if Marvel and DC can have their own universes, Fortnite has more than earned the right to one). From in-game terms to the lingo Fortnite fans have made their own, knowing how to "speak Fortnite" isn't just helpful, it's part of the fun. So buckle up - it's time to level up your vocab and learn the language of the island.

90s: One of the fastest ways to take the high ground in a build fight. Pulling off clean 90s takes skill and speed, but if you can master it, you're nearly unbeatable when it comes to getting above your opponent.

Aimbot: Literally, this refers to hackers and cheaters who use a program that provides perfect aim. But since Epic quickly hunts those players down and bans them (rightfully so), you'll probably hear it used jokingly to really great players with aim so good they might as well be a robot.

ADS: Short for "aim down sights." This is when you zoom in while aiming to make your shots more accurate - super helpful for long-range fights or when you want to make sure every bullet counts.

Bait: Setting a trap... Fortnite Style. Maybe you leave behind some tempting loot in the open and wait nearby, ready to laser the next person who tries to grab it. Or maybe you build something that looks safe... but isn't. If you're tricking someone into walking into danger, that's baiting.

Bandies: Quick slang for Bandages. They won't fully heal you, but they're better than nothing when your health's running low.

Battle Bus: The flying, balloon-powered bus that kicks off every match. It carries you and the rest of the players from Spawn Island to the main island.

Big Pot: Short for the Rare Shield Potion - the big blue bottle that gives you 50 Shield. Always a good find, especially early on.

Blue: If a teammate says they're blue, it means they've taken Shield damage. They still have health left, but their Shield bar just got chunked.

Bloom: When you fire a weapon, the bullets don't always go in a perfect line - that spread is called bloom. The more bloom, the less accurate the shot. You'll notice it most when spraying with ARs or SMGs.

BM: Short for "bad manners." Usually refers to unsportsmanlike stuff, like breakdancing on someone's body right after eliminating them.

Bot: Literally, a bot is an islander that is controlled by AI - the game deploys some of these to fill up spots in low-player matches, and they're pretty easy to take down since the AI isn't all that sophisticated. But the term is also used to bag on real players who play poorly (i.e., like dodgy AI).

Buff: When something gets a boost (more damage, faster speed, better stats) that's a buff. Updates sometimes buff underused weapons to make them more competitive.

Bunny Hop: A jumping trick that helps you move a bit faster than just running. Time it right and you'll be hopping your way across the island, and maybe dodging a few bullets too.

Camper: A player who hides most of the game, waiting to ambush someone when they least expect it. The classic version? Sitting in a bush all match and jumping out at just the right moment.

Cracked: If someone's cracked, they're landing shots, building fast, and just overall crushing it. It can also mean you've broken an enemy's Shield, so if you yell "Cracked them!" mid-match, your squad knows that player's wide open.

Crown Wins: Score a Victory Royale while wearing a Victory Crown, and it counts as a Crown Win. The more you collect, the more bragging rights you earn.

Default: A Default is someone using just the standard Recruit outfit; no fancy skins or cosmetics.

Downed: When your HP hits zero but you're not out yet; you're crawling around, praying for a revival from your teammate or mercy from your assailant. Also known as being "knocked."

Full Send: No holding back. When someone goes full send, they're going all-in on a fight: pushing hard, building fast, and trying to finish things quick.

GOAT: Stands for "Greatest Of All Time," and it's a big-time compliment. Originally from sports, this term caught on in Fortnite to hype up awesome players or moments. If someone says you're "goated," they mean you're absolutely legendary.

Harry Pottered: Trapped under a staircase in the middle of a build battle? Congrats, Boy Wizard, you've been Harry Pottered.

Hot Drop: A super popular landing spot right off the Battle Bus. Expect chaos, tons of loot, and a whole bunch of players fighting to survive the first few seconds.

Lasered: Getting hit with scary-accurate shots, usually in rapid fire. If someone says they got "lasered," it means they were melted in seconds by a player who didn't miss.

LeBron's House: Any house on the map that comes with its own basketball court. If it's got a hoop, it's LeBron's House.

Loadout: Your personal gear lineup. As you explore the island, you'll collect weapons, healing items, and tools - and the combo you roll with is your loadout. A good loadout can make or break your match.

Mats: Short for "materials": wood, brick, and metal. You gather these to build ramps, walls, boxes, and anything else you need to out-build or outlast the enemy.

Meds: Slang for healing items that boost your HP (your health bar). Doesn't include Shield items - those are a whole other (blue) beast.

Minis: Quick way of saying "Small Shield Potions." These are the fast-heal blue bottles that give you 25 Shield (but they only work if your Shield is sub-50).

Nerf: When an item, weapon, or feature gets toned down in an update, it's been nerfed.

Noob: Short for "newbie," this is someone who's brand new to the game and still figuring things out. It's often used teasingly, but hey, everyone's a noob at some point.

No Scope: Landing a shot with a sniper without zooming in. If you hit one of these, welcome to the highlight reel, buddy.

OG: Short for "original." This can mean a player who's been around since the early days of Chapter 1, or it can refer to classic items, places, or lore from Fortnite's beginning. In-game, OG is also the name of a car brand and the default Glider from the original seasons.

Skin: While Fortnite officially calls them Outfits, lots of players use "Skin" because that's the term used in tons of other games too. Same thing, different name.

One/One-Shot: A super common callout that means someone's just one hit away from being eliminated. If you hear "He's one!", it's time to chase.

OP: Stands for "Overpowered." If something is way stronger than it probably should be (looking at you, Infinity Blade), then it's OP. If it's really out of control (looking at you again, Infinity Blade)? Players will call it "broken."

Ping: To ping something means to mark it on the map or in the world, like pointing out loot, an enemy, or where to head next. Super useful for fast team communication without saying a word.

Pubs: Short for "Public Match." This just means you're playing the standard Battle Royale or Zero Build modes, not Arena or other competitive playlists. Most Fortnite games happen in pubs.

Quick Scope: When you flick to ADS (aim down sights) just for a second to line up your shot and fire fast. Great for getting accurate sniper hits without fully locking in.

Ready Up: Before you can jump into a match with your squad, you need to hit that "Ready" button. When enough players in your party are readied up, the game begins.

Rez: Short for "Resurrect", you'll probably hear this screamed into your ear by a knocked teammate as a polite request to be revived.

Tagged: If you say "I got tagged," you took damage. If you say "I tagged them," you landed a hit.

Turtling: Going full defense mode. Whether you're boxing up to heal or building a fort to wait things out, turtling is all about protection and patience.

Shield Pop: Breaking through someone's Shield with a shot or an explosion. If you hear "I popped their Shield," that enemy's now running on just health.

Vaulted: Sometimes items, weapons, or vehicles get removed from the game to make space for new ones. When that happens, they're "vaulted." They might come back one day... or not.

W Key Warrior: A player who pushes every fight, full speed ahead. The name comes from the W key on a computer keyboard (the one that moves you forward). These players never back down... even when they probably should.

PREVIOUSLY, ON FORTNITE...

Fortnite's transformation has been absolutely wild - some DNA remains, but it's basically a completely different universe at this point. What chapter marked your battle bus debut?

CHAPTER 1

Island Name: Athena
Start: October 2017

Here's where the legend began, even though nobody was calling it "Chapter 1" back then - that naming system came way later. We're talking Seasons 1 through X, the foundation era that started it all. Picture the most stripped-down version of Fortnite you can imagine: simple loot pools, basic transportation, and one single map called Athena that everyone learned by heart.

This era introduced the building blocks that define Fortnite today. Battle Passes and V-Bucks became the standard, but the real magic happened when Epic decided to blow everyone's minds with live storytelling. June 2018's Rocket Launch during Season 4 wasn't just an event - it was the moment Fortnite proved games could be interactive movies.

From that point forward, reality started bending in increasingly ridiculous ways. Space-time got involved because apparently normal battle royale wasn't exciting enough. The whole thing crescendoed with The End, an event so intense it literally deleted the game and replaced it with a black hole that had millions of players just... staring at their screens for hours.

CHAPTER 2

Island Name: Apollo
Start: October 2019

Welcome to the era that flipped everything upside down. When that black hole finally spit out a brand new world, players discovered Apollo - an island that made water actually matter for the first time, and had its very own dwellers; wildlife and characters.

Apollo lived through some serious drama during its lifespan. Season 3 basically turned the whole place into Atlantis when massive floods swallowed huge chunks of the map. But islands are resilient, apparently - the water eventually receded, and then things got prehistoric when Season 6 decided to throw everyone back to caveman times with a full multiverse reset.

Just when players thought they'd seen everything, Season 7 brought extraterrestrial visitors who definitely didn't come in peace. Then the Cube Queen showed up to make everyone's lives complicated, leading to yet another reality-ending finale. Because at this point, why wouldn't there be another apocalyptic ending followed by... you guessed it... a completely different island?

CHAPTER 3

Island Name: Artemis
Start: December 2021

Chapter 3 was short but sweet. The Rock kicked off this chapter because apparently that's just how Fortnite rolls now - with Dwayne Johnson leading the Foundation and flipping Apollo literally upside down to reveal Artemis on the other side. This frozen wasteland slowly defrosted as seasons passed, creating a completely different vibe from the chaos that came before.

Think of Chapter 3 as Fortnite's attempt at therapy after all those reality-breaking disasters.

Season 3 was literally called "Vibin'" which pretty much tells you everything about the mood Epic was going for. Instead of weekly apocalypses, players could actually relax and enjoy the game without constantly wondering if their favorite landing spot would still exist tomorrow.

But while players were busy enjoying this peaceful era, something called Chrome started creeping across the island like metallic quicksand. By the time anyone noticed this mysterious liquid coating everything, it was way too late to do anything about it...

CHAPTER 4

Island Name: Asteria
Start: December 2022

Reality had a breakdown and decided to mash together leftover pieces from Apollo and Artemis to create Asteria (hey, we've all been there). All this dimensional chaos meant the island couldn't keep its story straight, leading to wild Rift Encounters and Reality Augments that completely changed how battles played out.

One minute you're grinding rails through neon-soaked futuristic districts, the next you're riding a T-Rex through ancient forests like you're starring in your own action movie. Asteria didn't just have variety - it had an identity crisis that somehow made everything more exciting.

The real plot twist came with Season OG, when Epic basically said "remember when things were simple?" and brought back the Chapter 1 experience (for Seasons 5 to X). Players got to relive the glory days on classic Athena, but this nostalgic trip had consequences. When that familiar Zero Point black hole opened up again, it didn't just end the throwback season - it created a portal to escape to yet another completely different world.

CHAPTER 5

Island Name: Hellios
Start: December 2023

Epic didn't just drop a new map with Chapter 5 - they basically rebuilt the entire game engine. Wall climbing became a thing, animations got a major glow-up, and weapon customization through mods completely changed how loadouts worked.

The whole Greek mythology angle kicked off when Pandora's Box showed up and unleashed ancient chaos across Helios. Suddenly players were battling it out with Mount Olympus looming overhead and literal Underworld portals scattered around the island. Gods, monsters, and battle royales apparently make a pretty solid combination.

Then Epic pulled one of their signature reality shifts, catapulting everyone from ancient mythological landscapes straight into the post-apocalyptic wasteland of Season 3's "Wrecked." This time around, vehicle customization took center stage for the first time ever, letting players soup up their rides to survive the harsh new world.

When Doctor Doom destroyed everything with Pandora's Box (a lot of crossover going on here), players got to dip back into a Chapter 2 Remix (officially denoted as Chapter 5: Season 5), before we moved onto something entirely new.

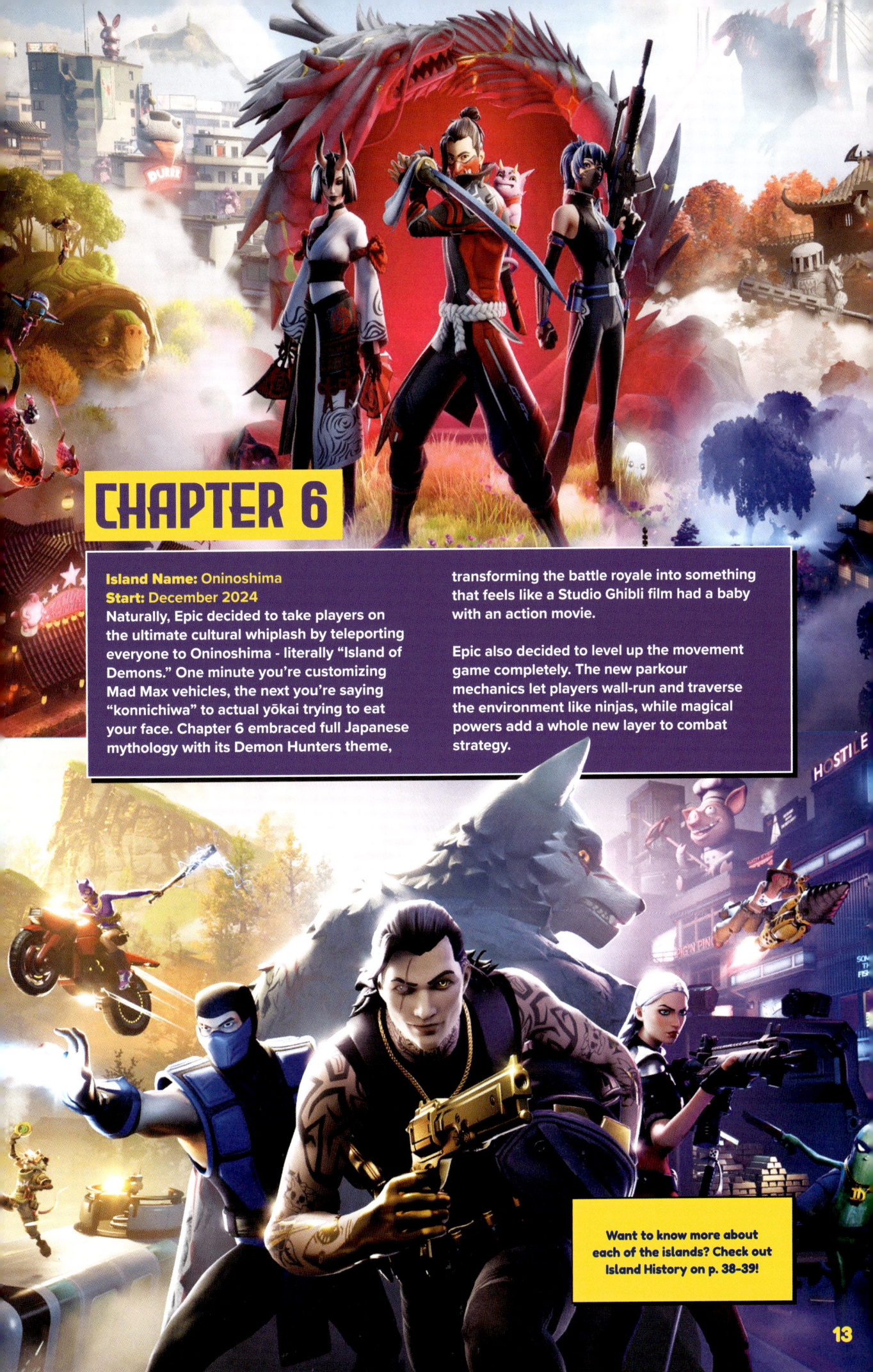

CHAPTER 6

Island Name: Oninoshima
Start: December 2024

Naturally, Epic decided to take players on the ultimate cultural whiplash by teleporting everyone to Oninoshima - literally "Island of Demons." One minute you're customizing Mad Max vehicles, the next you're saying "konnichiwa" to actual yōkai trying to eat your face. Chapter 6 embraced full Japanese mythology with its Demon Hunters theme, transforming the battle royale into something that feels like a Studio Ghibli film had a baby with an action movie.

Epic also decided to level up the movement game completely. The new parkour mechanics let players wall-run and traverse the environment like ninjas, while magical powers add a whole new layer to combat strategy.

Want to know more about each of the islands? Check out Island History on p. 38–39!

GAME MODES

Long gone are the days where you drop into a round of battle royale by default. Long gone. That's vanilla now - you can have the whole banana split these days.

Okay, so that metaphor may have ended shakily, but how else would you explain that Fortnite went from one core base mode to around ten? Fortnite grew from a game to a platform, offering different experiences for players to pick, choose, and even make.

Battle Royale is Fortnite's core game mode, where players (and the occasional bot; no one's perfect) are dropped onto an ever-shrinking island, forced to fight to the death to be the last one standing. She may be vanilla, but she's a classic, and Epic will never leave her behind; this mode sees the most updates, and is also home to the game's absolutely wild storyline and lore.

Zero Build has all the elements of the classic mode, but without any building. While this takes mats and structure off of your plate, it ultimately makes the game a bit more deadly - amping up the importance of map awareness and 1v1 duelling.

Save the World was the very first game mode developed; in fact, it was supposed to be the main one. Battle Royale was just a little add-on to tide players over. Alas, how times have changed. But Save the World is still chugging along, providing a PvE mode that pits players against in-game monsters instead of each other. Same Storm, same survival - different game.

Creative is the mode for the budding game devs out there, giving them access to the tools to build their very own Fortnite experience for players all over the world to play. Try your hand at making your own game, or cruise player-made creations to find something new to test out.

Fortnite OG knows that sometimes it's nice to just return to a simpler time, when the island first dropped. This mode brings back Chapter 1 realness, letting players enjoy classic locations, iconic weapons and a nice heavy dose of nostalgia.

Reload is a lightning-fast 40-player, squads-only Battle Royale where teamwork is everything. Death isn't the end - it's just the beginning, as fallen teammates can quickly rejoin the fight. This mode strips away the slower elements of traditional BR for pure, non-stop action.

Ballistic brings tactical FPS gameplay to Fortnite with intense 5v5 round-based matches played entirely in first-person. It's Fortnite's answer to competitive shooters like VALORANT and CS2, complete with precise gunplay and strategic team coordination.

Festival transforms Fortnite into a full-blown rhythm game experience, channeling serious Guitar Hero vibes. Rock out to chart-toppers from superstars like Lady Gaga, Sabrina Carpenter, Billie Eilish and tons of other artists. Perfect your timing and feel the beat!

LEGO Fortnite reimagines the entire Fortnite universe in colorful brick form. Whether you want to survive against the elements or build your dream world, this family-friendly mode lets creativity run wild in a charming block-based adventure.

Rocket Racing delivers high-octane vehicular mayhem with extensive customization options. Build your dream ride, master the tracks, and leave your opponents in the dust across a variety of challenging courses.

HEALTH & SHIELDS

Pointing and shooting is only half the battle; keeping yourself alive is what actually wins games. Health and Shield management can make or break your Victory Royale chances. You don't get sent back to the lobby because your aim was off or your builds were wonky - you get sent back when that health bar hits zero.

RESTORING HP

Epic loves throwing weird healing methods at us every season (seriously, who thought crouching in sketchy pipe water was a good idea?), but there are some reliable healing options that show up pretty consistently.

Bandages: The OG healing item that's been patching up players since day one. These common finds give you a quick +15 HP boost (capping at 75 HP) in just 3 seconds. They're nothing fancy, but perfect for topping off after minor scrapes. Just don't expect them to save you from serious damage, that's like trying to fix a car crash with duct tape.

Medkits: Think of these as bandages on steroids: they'll restore you to full health, but at the cost of a painfully long 10-second animation. Ten seconds might not sound like much, but when you're getting third-partied or the Storm's breathing down your neck, it feels like an eternity. Save medkits for those rare moments when you've got solid cover and actual breathing room.

These are less common than bandies and medkits, but these two methods also come in and out of the Vault pretty regularly:

Med-Mists: Chapter 3's game-changing healing item that works on everyone: your squad, hired NPCs, and even enemies if you're feeling charitable. It ticks for 5 HP at a time up to 150 total, but the real magic is that you can use it while doing literally anything else. Running from the storm? Healing. Sliding down a mountain? Still healing. It's clutch for those panic moments when you need health but can't afford to stop moving.

Camping: Nothing beats setting up shop at a tent or campfire for some serious R&R with your squad. Tents heal you at 5 HP per second with no cap, so you can literally chill until you're back to full health. Plus, the whole squad can benefit from camping heals together; it's like a cozy healing party in the middle of chaos.

Some seasons have AI critters (like Chapter 6's Water Sprite) or Characters that can patch you up. For Characters, it's usually in exchange for some Gold. The Character changes with the storyline, but they're usually rocking that classic red and white medical aesthetic, so keep an eye out for anyone looking like they raided a first aid kit for their outfit.

RESTORING SHIELDS

Shields are absolutely non-negotiable for any serious Fortnite player. That blue bar is your lifeline - a buffer zone that soaks up damage before it touches your precious health. Getting Shield should be one of your first priorities after landing, and keeping it maxed should stay important right until you're claiming that Victory Royale.

 **Small Shield Potion:** AKA Minis, the MVP of shield items. They give you 25 Shield Points (capping at 50 SP) in just 2 seconds, making them perfect for quick mid-fight top-ups. Sure, they won't give you full shield, but their lightning-fast consumption means you can pop them almost anywhere without much risk.

 **Shield Potion:** AKA Big Pots, granting a hefty 50 Shield Points with no cap limit, but there's a catch: that 5-second chug time makes you a sitting duck. Save these for when you've got solid cover and breathing room. If you absolutely must use one during a fight, make sure you're locked down behind some serious protection first.

DOUBLE DUTY

Some items pull double duty and restore both Health and Shields. These items are clutch, but they tend not to be in play as much as the single-speciality items. If you're lucky and playing a season that has a double duty in there, it's likely to be:

Chug Jug: The Chug Jug maxes out both health and shield in one go. It takes 10 seconds total to use (with a 2-second wind-up), providing steady healing that restores 10 health per half-second tick. The good news is you can move while using it, so you're not completely defenseless. You can also throw it to teammates by holding aim and using the projectile arc. It's incredibly powerful but risky - that 10-second commitment makes you vulnerable, so most players build cover or find a safe spot before chugging.

Chug Splash: These throwable healing bottles use the same projectile arc as grenades, creating a 1-tile splash zone when they hit the ground. They restore +20 Effective Health, which basically means +20 to whichever you need most (Health or Shields). Just like Med-Mists, they'll heal anyone in the splash zone, including enemies, so watch where you're throwing unless you want to accidentally patch up your opponents.

PRODUCE BOXES

The island's packed with more... let's call them "organic" healing options? I mean, glowing mushrooms and slurp-infused fruit aren't exactly what you'd find in your backyard, but they're natural by Fortnite standards. These foraged heals might not pack the punch of your traditional bandages or potions, but they work instantly with about a 1-second pickup time, making them perfect for quick health boosts when you're constantly on the move.

 Apples: Give 5 HP and grow in orchards or anywhere you spot fruit trees.

 Bananas: Another 5 HP option hanging around palm trees in tropical zones.

 Cabbages: Pack 10 HP and grow in farmland areas - look for those neat crop rows.

 Coconuts: The versatile option at 5 HP/Shield, found near palm trees in beachy areas.

 Corn: Another farmland crop that restores 10 HP when you need a quick boost.

 Meat: The heavyweight at 15 HP, but you'll need to hunt down some island wildlife first.

 Mushrooms: Your shield savior at 5 Shield per mushroom, growing in dark forest and swamp areas. Best part? No cap limit, so eat every single one you find for maximum shield.

 Peppers: Not only heal 5 HP but give you a sweet 20% speed boost for a full minute - perfect for Storm runs.

 Slurpshrooms: The premium forage option at 10 HP/Shield, tucked away in swampy regions.

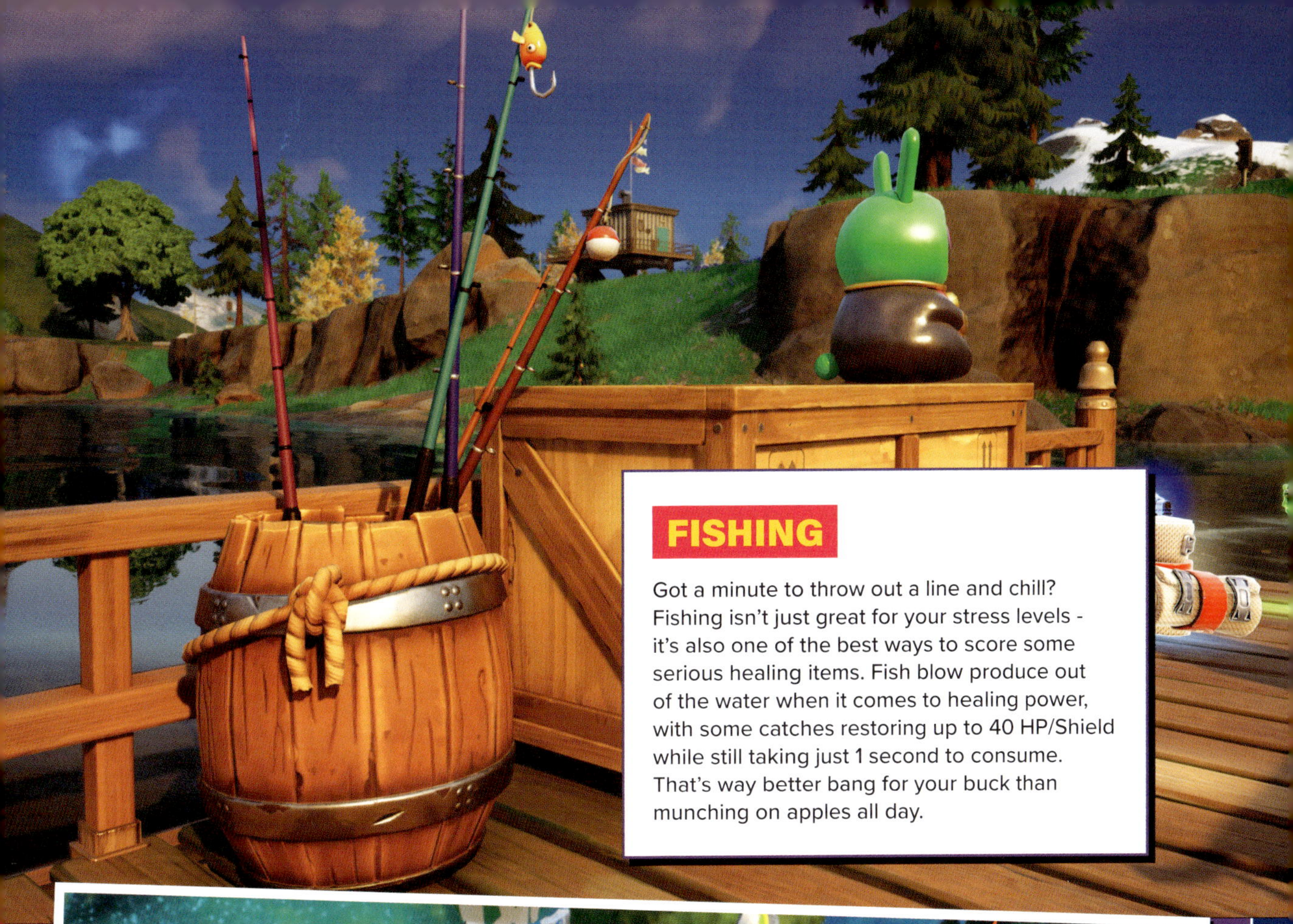

FISHING

Got a minute to throw out a line and chill? Fishing isn't just great for your stress levels - it's also one of the best ways to score some serious healing items. Fish blow produce out of the water when it comes to healing power, with some catches restoring up to 40 HP/Shield while still taking just 1 second to consume. That's way better bang for your buck than munching on apples all day.

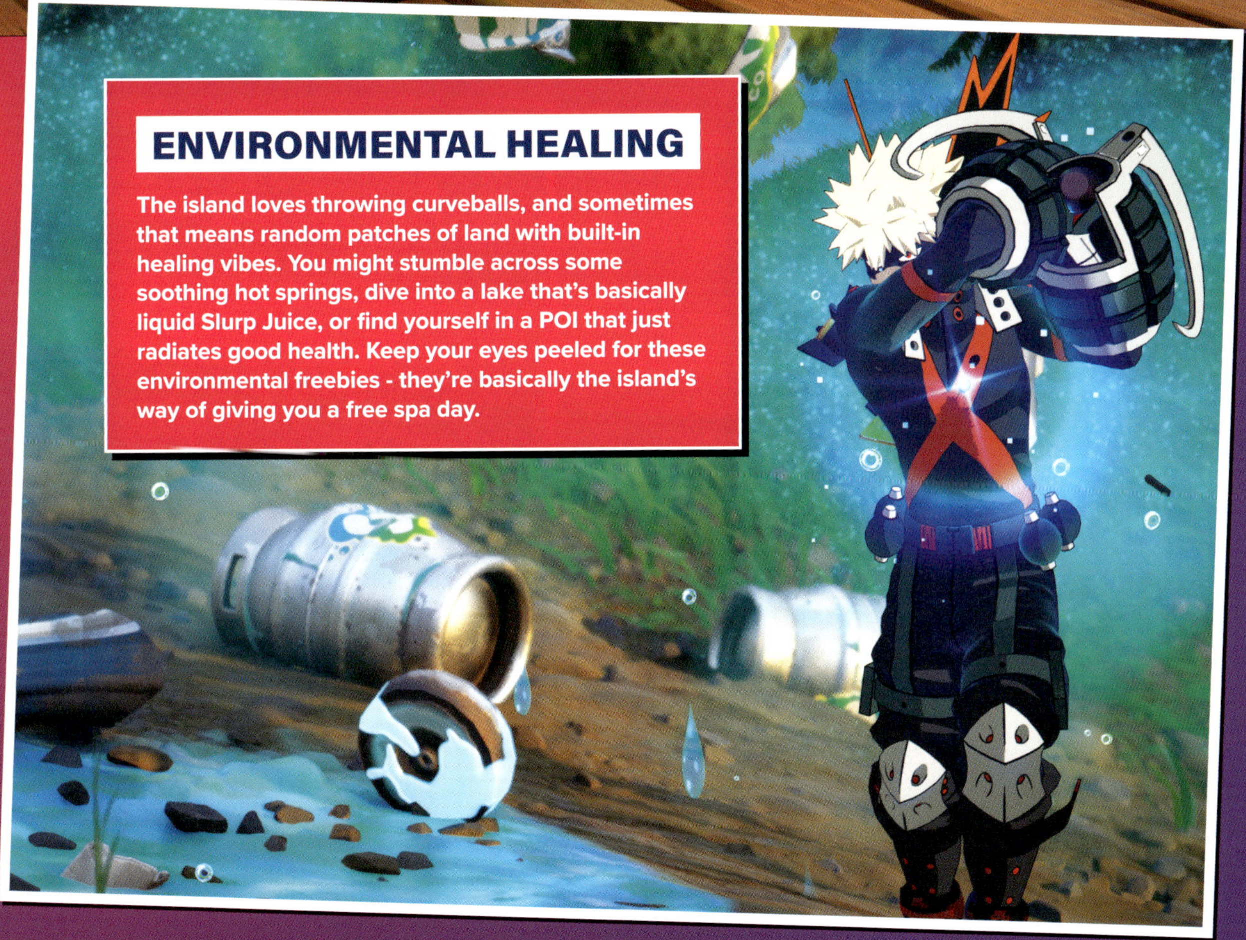

ENVIRONMENTAL HEALING

The island loves throwing curveballs, and sometimes that means random patches of land with built-in healing vibes. You might stumble across some soothing hot springs, dive into a lake that's basically liquid Slurp Juice, or find yourself in a POI that just radiates good health. Keep your eyes peeled for these environmental freebies - they're basically the island's way of giving you a free spa day.

Some weapons come with built-in healing perks that make them extra valuable. Superhero collab weapons are notorious for this - they'll deal damage to enemies while patching you up at the same time (like the now-vaulted Sideways Scythe giving you HP every time you eliminated opponents or AI enemies).

THE STORM

The Storm is the invisible hand that shapes every Battle Royale game. Without it, players would spread out across the entire island, hiding in corners until someone got bored enough to go looking for a fight. Think of it as nature's way of saying "Hey, stop camping in that bush and get moving!" The Storm forces all 100 players to get closer and closer together until there's an epic final showdown.

Let's be honest: between chasing Quests, chatting with Characters, dodging gunfire, and maybe getting a space slug stuck on your face, it's easy to forget the Storm's still out to get you. But trust - The Storm wants you off that island, ASAP.

The Storm demands timing, strategy and quick-paced decision-making. Do you rotate early and secure good positioning? Do you risk staying longer to grab better loot? Do you fight the squad rotating late, or do you let them pass?

Did you know the Storm is sentient? Originally, players thought the Storm was being controlled by the Imagined Order. But then Epic revealed that the Storm actually has a will of its own (despite being an extension of Storm Kings), and it is an entity wielded by the Fortnite's Biggest Bad Faction: The Last Reality.

STORY OF THE STORM

Back in Fortnite's early days, the Storm worked a bit differently than it does today. The original Storm was pretty basic – it just moved in, dealt damage, and that was that. But Epic Games kept tweaking and improving it to make matches more exciting.

In the beginning, players figured out they could just hide in The Storm and heal themselves with bandages and med kits, so Epic made the Storm deal more damage over time. Throughout different seasons and chapters, The Storm has gotten some pretty interesting iterations:

- **Storm Surge:** Storm Surge kicks in when too many players are alive for the current circle. Instead of time-based damage, it targets players who've dealt the least damage to opponents.
- **Storm Sickness:** Stay in The Storm too long and you'll get Storm Sickness, which prevents you from healing for several seconds after reaching safety. This stops players from tanking Storm damage and immediately healing up once they're safe.

The Storm will damage all players, animals, characters and AI within it, but cannot damage structures or vehicles.

STORM STRATEGY

- Everyone's funneling toward safety at the same time, which means the zone edges become elimination buffets. Get there early, find a good angle, and capitalize on desperate runners being predictable and distracted.
- But if you can't get to a safe zone early, then stay vigilant. It can be easy to focus on outrunning the purple haze and forget that other players are also likely running for safety, so be ready for an ambush around the edges of the eye - or a sniper who might be waiting to welcome you to the bubble.
- The Storm can actually be your ally when fighting bosses. Timing a boss fight during a shrinking circle could let the Storm chip away at the boss's health, dealing additional damage to your own offense. It's risky as it would require you to stock up on healing items beforehand and to have an exit strategy in place should things go south, but it can make bosses go down a whole lot faster.

SURVIVAL GUIDE
WILDLIFE

The island doesn't just have 99 players, henchmen and a malevolent sentient storm that's trying to kill you - there's a whole ecosystem of creatures that want a piece of the action too. Wildlife crashed the party in Chapter 2 and have been stirring up trouble ever since.

THE ROTATING PETTING ZOO

Epic Games treats animals exactly like they treat everything else in Fortnite - here today, vaulted tomorrow. One season you're dodging aggressive boars and getting chased by wolf packs. The next season brings magical spirit sprites or zombie chickens that just won't quit.

The wildlife roster changes constantly, which keeps matches unpredictable. Sometimes you'll find friendly creatures you can actually tame and ride into battle, other times you'll stumble into a pack of hungry predators while you're trying to heal up. There's no telling what kind of creatures you'll bump into, but some critters are definitely Epic's favourites and are more often in play than not.

CHICKEN

HP: 60
Damage: 1

Don't let their fluffy appearance fool you - chickens are surprisingly useful! These feathered friends normally mind their own business and run away when they see you coming. But grab one and hold it above your head, and suddenly you've got a makeshift glider that slows your fall. Plus, chickens make decent weapons if you get close enough to smack enemies with them.

Attack a chicken and it might get mad enough to fight back. Most chickens drop meat when eliminated, but keep an eye out for the special glowing ones. Orange and purple chickens are basically walking loot boxes that drop legendary or epic weapons when you take them out. You can even find chickens stuck in broken vending machines sometimes.

FROG

HP: 250
Damage: 15

Good luck catching these slippery little guys! Frogs are the speed demons of the animal kingdom - they'll hop away faster than you can say "ribbit." They don't have much health, so one good hit usually does the trick, but actually landing that hit is the real challenge.

Frogs are completely harmless and just want to escape, but they drop meat when eliminated. They're more of a quick snack opportunity than a serious gameplay element, assuming you can actually catch one.

WOLF

HP: 20
Damage: N/A

Wolves are the apex predators of the island and they travel in packs of three or more. Unlike other animals, wolves will actively hunt you down and attack on sight. But here's the cool part - you can actually tame them and turn them into your personal bodyguards.

Tamed wolves will follow you around, attack your enemies, and you can even ride them like a furry motorcycle. They're faster than boars and raptors, making them excellent for quick rotations. When eliminated, wolves drop three meat instead of one, and the glowing orange and purple ones drop legendary or epic weapons.

SURVIVAL GUIDE
ISLAND DWELLERS

NPCs showed up in Chapter 2: Season 5 and have been part of every season since. These AI characters spawn at set locations around the map and actually talk to you, unlike regular enemies. Chat with them and they'll get added to your Character Collection Book.

CHARACTER TYPES

There are five different character types in Battle Royale, though they are also treated like weapons and items and shuffled in-and-out of the Vault depending on the season:

- **Neutral:** The most common type. These characters will trade services for Bars and engage in dialogue with players. Attack them and they'll fight back.
- **Static:** Technically characters but really just interactive machines like Bounty Boards, Upgrade Benches and Vending Machines that accept Bars for services.
- **Hostile:** Aggressive characters that attack players immediately, similar to IO Guards or Boss AI. They typically drop high-tier loot when defeated.
- **Healer:** Characters offering single dialogue lines who let players mimic their emotes in exchange for regular Chug Splash healing effects.
- **Phones:** Similar to static objects but exclusively used for initiating quests.

Characters spawn in their specific spot every time a match kicks off. If you're looking for someone specific and another player has got to them first, don't worry - you can still interact with their ghostly form after they've been defeated.

The island's very first Character was Bandolette, the unrivaled ambush predator of the jungle.

CHARACTER INTERACTIONS

Different Characters offer various interaction options. Like most Fortnite features, these services also rotate in and out of the vault while new ones get added:

 Duel: Challenge them to combat and claim their weapon as a prize.

 Patch Up: Purchase a small health restoration.

 Prop Disguise: Transform into a prop object for stealth tactics.

 Rift: Open a sky rift for gliding to new locations.

 Conversation: Have a little chat.

 Hire: Pay to recruit the character as your fighting companion.

Every hireable Character has their own combat speciality: Heavy Specialists bring additional firepower thanks to cluster bombs. Scout Specialists roam the area to spot (and ping) nearby enemies and chests before you do. Medic Specialists will keep a helpful eye on your HP. Supply Specialists ensure you're well stocked with ammo, mats and heals.

GIMME GOLD

Want to use these services? You'll need Bars - Fortnite's gold currency. Eliminate other players or NPCs, loot chests and safes, hit up cash registers, or complete bounties from Bounty Boards (look for the weapon scope symbol on your map). No Bars, no service.

CHARACTER CROSSWORD

There have been hundreds of Characters that have graced the island with their presence, but some truly iconic ones have stayed in our hearts... and Fortnite lore. Can you guess the legendary Fortnite characters from the clues and complete the crossword? Check out p. 62-63.

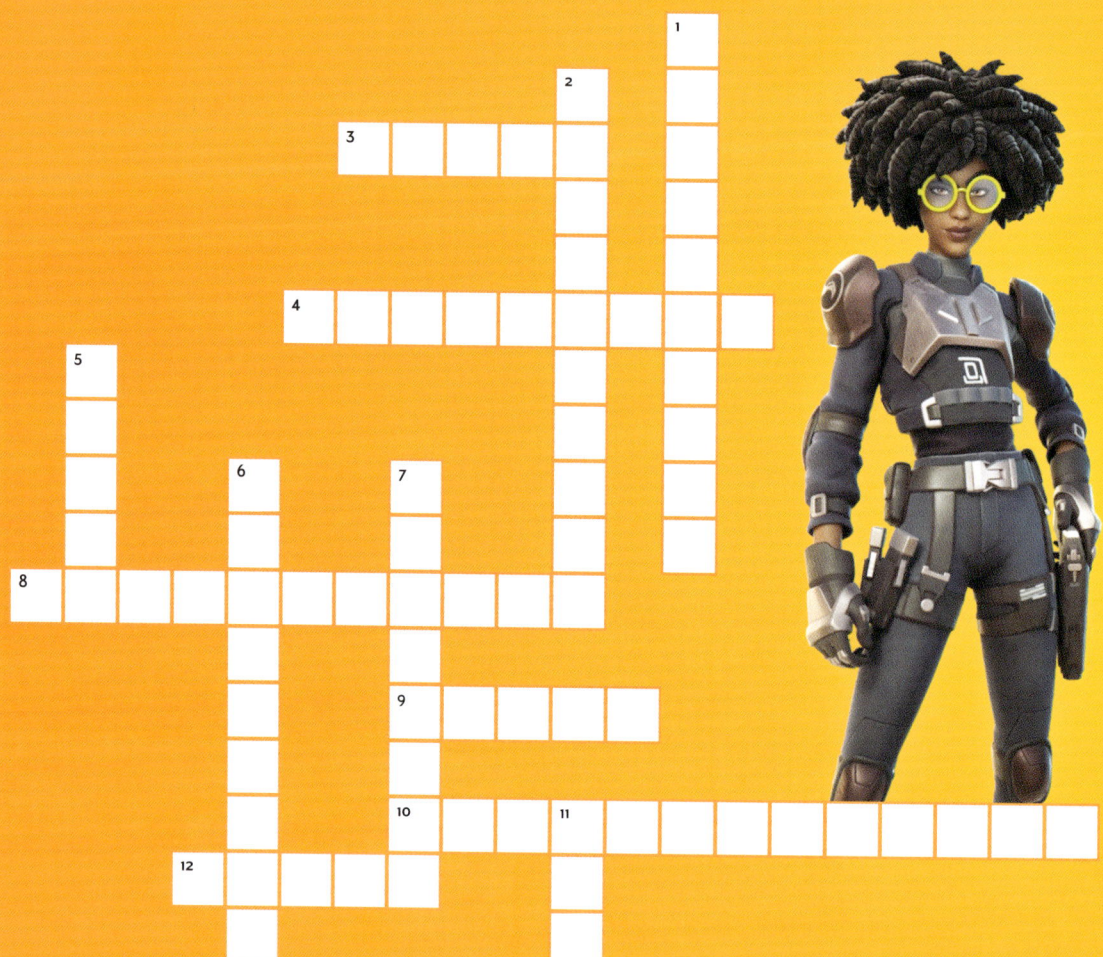

Across

3. This fencer was a member of the Society before turning good. (5)
4. The blond-haired, multiple titled, OG face of Fortnite. (4, 5)
8. This genius inventor was a big bad before she turned good in Chapter 4. (6, 5)
9. Everything this criminal touches turns to gold. (5)
10. Can you smell what the leader of the Seven is cookin'? (3, 10)
12. Kinda quiet. Bruises easily. (5)

Down

1. This cheerleader is truly a beauty and a (storm) beast. (6, 4)
2. The very first NPC to roam the island. (10)
5. The Mask Maker and ruler of the Thousand Faces citadel. (5)
6. This calico is a secret agent and pet food entrepreneur. (9)
7. This pink-haired bandit had you praying for a hold up. (8)
11. This beloved aquatic critter died in the arms of Batman. (9)

SPOT THE DIFFERENCE

Can you spot the differences between these two pictures? There are eight differences in total.
Check out p. 62-63 for answers.

THE ARMORY

You can bush camp and third-party your way into the final circle, but eventually the music stops and it's time to dance. Those last few opponents aren't going to eliminate themselves, so if you want that Victory Royale crown sitting pretty on your head, you're going to need to get comfortable pulling a trigger or two.

Whether you're a master marksman or up-close-and-personal slugger, Fortnite's weapon pool has something for you. The in-game arsenal is mammoth, and with new gear dropping every season (while classics get vaulted and unvaulted faster than you can say "mythic"), it seems impossible to keep track of every single weapon in the game.

But you don't need to - you just need to master your knowledge of a few main concepts to keep on top of things. So let's break down everything you need to know about Fornit's ever-changing arsenal.

AMMO

Every shooter needs bullets, and Fortnite's no exception. Assault rifles, shotguns, snipers - they all have their preferred diet of destruction, and it's up to you to know what to feed them.

Ammo Type	Weapon Type	Effective Range	Damage Per Shot
Light Ammo	Pistols, SMGs	Close	Low
Medium Ammo	Pistols, Assault Rifles	Mid	Medium
Heavy Ammo	Sniper Rifles	Long	High
Shells	Shotguns	Close	High
Arrows	Bows, Crossbows	Mid	Low
Rockets	Explosives	Mid/Long	Very High

Ammo is everywhere if you know where to look. Pop open chests, crack into those dedicated ammo boxes scattered around POIs, and keep your eyes peeled for supply drops when they're part of the seasonal rotation. Sometimes you'll even stumble across loose rounds just chilling on the ground. Running out of bullets during a heated build battle or final circle showdown is the kind of rookie mistake that'll send you straight back to the lobby, so always grab more than you think you need.

RARITIES

Fortnite's weapon rarity system follows the same six-tier structure as every other item in the game. Higher rarity means better stats across the board, but also means you'll be competing with everyone else who wants to get their hands on that legendary-tier firepower.

COMMON	UNCOMMON	RARE	EPIC	LEGENDARY	MYTHIC	EXOTIC

A rarer weapon deals more damage than lower-tiered weapons in the same category, but not necessarily more than a weapon in a different category. Don't throw away a solid shotgun just because you stumbled across a legendary pistol. Smart players consider DPS and effective range when building their loadout, because having the right tool for each situation beats having the prettiest collection of high-tier gear that doesn't work together.

Mythic and Exotic weapons can be found in chests on rare occasions, but they're more often found by eliminating AI or purchasing from Characters.

UPGRADING

You don't have to rely on luck to find yourself a rare shooter. You can actually pump up your favorite weapon's tier (and damage output) by spending some Gold Bars.

There are two upgrade methods that exist in-game, and Epic loves keeping us on our toes by switching between them when seasons or chapters roll over. Always double-check which system is currently active before you go hunting for upgrades:

Mod Benches: These mechanical stations are scattered across the island, with the highest concentration around POIs and major landmarks. Just make sure you've got the weapon you want to boost equipped before you interact with the bench.

NPCs: Occasionally, friendly NPCs will offer upgrade services as part of their repertoire. This method tends to be less common than the benches, so don't bank on finding it everywhere.

Whether it's benches or characters, the currency is always the same: Gold Bars.
That common-to-uncommon bump might be pocket change, but pushing a weapon to legendary status will seriously dent your wallet.

Rarity Update	Gold Bars
Common >> Uncommon	200
Uncommon >> Rare	300
Rare >> Epic	400
Epic >> Legendary	500

If upgrade costs are looking steep, you can also snag some high rarity weapons straight from Vending Machines. A flat 50 Gold Bars for premium gear is way more palatable than the escalating upgrade fees, especially when you're working with a tight budget and need that firepower fast.

WEAPON TYPES

Epic's weapon designers love getting creative, but underneath all the flashy effects and unique mechanics, every piece of firepower falls into these time-tested categories that have anchored Fortnite's arsenal from the very start.

ASSAULT RIFLES

These workhorses handle most situations with ease, delivering consistent damage across medium to long distances while packing enough magazine capacity for extended firefights. They're the backbone of any solid loadout for good reason.

Expect damage to weaken significantly beyond 50 meters, potentially dropping to just two-thirds of full power at maximum range.

Bloom will scatter your shots during rapid fire, so start each engagement with a precise first shot before letting loose with body shots as accuracy deteriorates.

SNIPER RIFLES

Purpose-built for cross-map eliminations, these powerhouses can end fights with a single well-placed shot. The catch? They demand surgical precision and excellent target prediction to be effective.

Always carry a close-quarters alternative since sniper rifles become liabilities when enemies close the gap.

Factor in bullet travel time and gravity when engaging moving opponents: shoot where they're headed, not where they currently stand.

PISTOLS

The dependable generalists of Fortnite's weapon roster, pistols handle close to medium-range encounters competently without excelling in any particular area. They're solid secondary options that complement specialized primary weapons.

Pistols that take Light Ammo have surprisingly tight hip fire spread, making them clutch in unexpected close encounters.

Pistol variants span different effective ranges and ammunition requirements, so be sure to know which type of pistol you're wielding before engaging.

SMGs

Unmatched in close-quarters destruction, these bullet hoses melt opponents at arm's length but become nearly worthless once distance enters the equation. Their spray patterns and rapid damage falloff make precision impossible at range.

Treat SMGs as cleanup tools: weaken enemies with other weapons, then close distance for the finishing blow.

Manage ammunition consumption and recoil through short, deliberate bursts rather than holding down the trigger.

SHOTGUNS

The go-to duel weapon - shotguns absolutely wreck opponents at close range with massive damage and forgiving spread patterns that don't require pixel-perfect aim. But just like SMGs, they're pretty much useless once you step back even to mid-range.

Pro tip: skip the full reload animation by keeping your shells topped off; partial reloads are way faster and keep you in the action.

Shotguns are a must-have for any face-to-face showdown where you need instant eliminations.

EXPLOSIVES

These bad boys are built for wrecking structures and vehicles, not chasing down individual players. Sure, they hit like trucks, but their sluggish fire rate leaves you wide open between shots.

One well-placed rocket at the foundation of a structure will have the whole thing come tumbling down.

Every explosive brings splash damage to the party, so whipping one out in tight spaces means you're eating some of your own damage too.

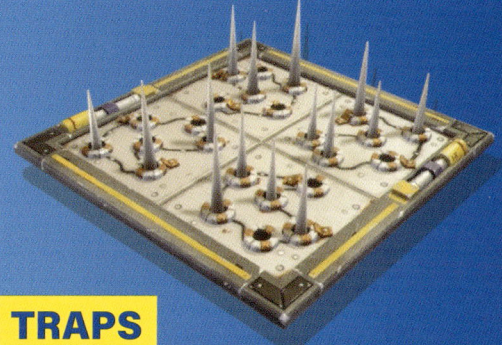

TRAPS

Perfect for playing defense and controlling space. Drop traps to protect your base or catch someone chasing you through a build battle. Think of them as your personal security system.

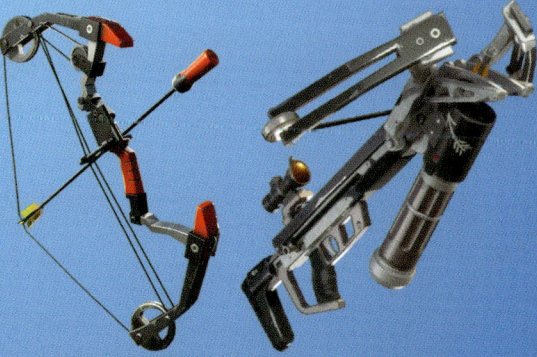

BOWS/CROSSBOWS

The Vault's favourite residents, these projectile weapons show up randomly across seasons in different flavors. Just like explosives, you'll need solid prediction skills to actually hit anything that's moving.

Pretty weak damage means they're basically useless against builds or beefier AI enemies. They use the same targeting arc system as throwables, so factor in gravity with every shot.

MELEE

The only weapons that never run out of ammo, which is both a blessing and a curse since you've got to get dangerously close to your target to actually use them. Most collab weapons are melee types: Michelangelo's Nunchakus, Shuri's Black Panther Claws, you name it - each bringing their own wild mechanics to close combat.

1v1 TIPS

Ready to claim that Victory Royale? Whether you're dropping hot for maximum chaos or playing it safe until the final showdown, nailing your 1v1 skills is absolutely crucial. The difference between heading back to the lobby and securing that crown often comes down to how well you handle those intense one-on-one moments.

MAX OUT YOUR LOADOUT

The island's packed with surprises: hostile players, bloodthirsty beasts, and who knows what other wild threats are lurking around every corner. You best be prepared or you'll find yourself back in the lobby, stat.

Here's the golden rule: optimize your loadout the second you hit the ground. Stick to the tried-and-true 2:2:1 formula: two weapons, two healing items, and one flex slot for whatever the situation demands. And in that order!

Your weapon combo should cover all ranges: grab a reliable mid-range option like an Assault Rifle, then pair it with something punchy for close encounters (Shotguns and Pistols are your best friends here). For heals, smaller items are clutch since they're faster to pop during those heated exchanges.

CLAIM THE HIGH GROUND

High ground = game over for your opponents. It's that simple. If Mother Nature didn't bless you with a hill, then it's time to get building. Even in cramped spaces where you can't tower up, stay mobile; keep jumping, keep moving, and remember to angle your shots downward.

Remember: High ground isn't just about height - it's about controlling angles and forcing your opponent into disadvantageous positions.

DEALING WITH HENCHMEN

Ever since Chapter 2, AI enemies have been stirring up trouble across the island. While PvE shares some DNA with PvP combat, there are definitely some unique strategies to master.

Those faction henchmen scattered around POIs? They're honestly more of a minor inconvenience than a real threat. Their AI is pretty basic, so a simple jump-and-shoot-down approach will clear them out quickly. Just don't let them third-party you during a real fight!

Use henchmen as early-game practice for your aim and movement—they're perfect for warming up your reflexes.

Learning boss attack patterns can give you a huge edge - most have predictable wind-ups that you can exploit for easy damage windows.

BOSS BATTLES

Now bosses? That's a whole different beast. These hulking threats pack serious stats and drop incredible loot, but they'll put up a real fight.

- Start every boss encounter with some long-range headshots. Most bosses roll with around 400 Shield and 100 HP, so softening them up from afar is always smart.
- If henchmen crash the party, shift focus immediately and wipe them out. Getting swarmed while trying to focus on a boss is a one-way ticket to the lobby.
- Bosses spawn once per match, making them hotspots for third-parties. Keep your head on a swivel; other players love to "help" clean up after boss fights.

General duelling tip: keep those APM (actions per minute) cranked up to eleven. Unpredictable movement makes you a nightmare to track, and that split-second advantage can make all the difference.

CROSSHAIR MATCH-UP

Ready to take your shot? Pick up your sniper rifle and take aim at the unsuspecting players down below - can you follow the shot from the crosshair to find its target?

Check out p. 62-63 for answers.

WEAPON WORDSEARCH

Fortnite's arsenal expands and shrinks every season, with new weapons introduced, past pieces put into the vault and the occasional old favourite that's dusted off and put back out into rotation. There are a ridiculous amount of arms in the game - can you find some of the game's weapons in the wordsearch below? Check out p. 62-63 for answers.

C	B	X	G	S	I	X	S	H	O	O	T	E	R	N	N	Y	K	S	S
S	A	V	A	T	K	O	W	A	Y	R	W	X	S	C	P	X	D	H	T
C	S	A	T	D	H	X	B	Z	O	D	N	H	P	C	P	W	Q	C	O
W	S	W	E	V	G	E	S	Z	R	L	N	B	D	N	U	S	P	S	R
E	B	U	K	C	F	F	D	U	E	L	F	I	R	E	R	I	P	S	M
D	O	Y	E	L	X	J	M	U	N	A	W	E	G	E	M	D	R	S	S
A	O	E	E	I	D	G	M	O	B	X	H	O	G	H	M	K	Z	I	C
N	S	O	P	Z	U	P	N	G	T	C	E	N	B	P	T	F	F	W	O
E	T	W	E	N	S	N	B	S	N	P	I	W	G	L	B	H	P	E	U
R	Q	W	R	B	A	I	V	U	O	L	Y	G	C	P	A	Z	A	H	T
G	P	U	P	C	G	A	A	R	C	J	Y	R	G	V	A	M	K	W	I
S	N	P	D	C	D	L	O	Y	D	D	N	K	K	Z	S	I	I	P	K
P	H	N	H	D	T	N	U	G	I	N	I	M	O	A	D	Q	N	R	O
C	A	I	W	E	C	O	M	B	A	T	S	H	O	T	G	U	N	G	P
H	L	K	K	B	O	O	G	I	E	B	O	M	B	Q	Y	V	M	D	L
L	F	C	E	D	A	L	B	Y	T	I	N	I	F	N	I	B	J	R	O
X	O	T	R	W	S	A	V	C	Z	E	X	W	Z	W	T	D	Y	L	T
R	X	J	F	R	G	Y	T	M	R	Q	G	C	C	F	G	D	O	X	S
M	R	N	E	K	D	S	Y	C	N	W	T	E	X	A	C	I	W	X	I
Z	E	X	I	T	W	M	Y	A	V	O	R	Y	O	P	R	V	I	J	P

Rocket Launcher	Drum Gun	Hand Cannon	Big Chill	Clingers
Combat Shotgun	Spire Rifle	Six Shooter	Minigun	Boogie Bomb
The Dub	Krypto	Night Hawk	Primal Bow	Bass Boost
Gatekeeper	Pistol	Storm Scout	Grenade	Infinity Blade

ISLAND HISTORY

The Fortnite Island has been through more glow-ups than a mythic weapon. It's been flipped, fractured, rebuilt, and rebooted - and every iteration brings new biomes, secrets, and chaos. From the dusty hills of Athena to the neon samurai vibes of Oninoshima, each island tells a different chapter of Fortnite's story. Some lasted for years, others just a single season, but all of them have left their mark on the Loop. Let's take a tour through the wild worlds we've battled in across the years.

ATHENA

Chapters: Chapter 1, Chapter 4: Season OG
First Release: September 2017
Athena is the very first island that introduced the concept of Fortnite's Battle Royale to players. We learned the ropes here, so she'll always have a special place in Fortnite players' hearts. Luckily, we can visit her any time now that we have OG Mode.

APOLLO

Chapters: Chapter 2, Chapter 5: Season 5 (Chapter 2 Remix)
First Release: October 2019
After Athena was canonically sucked into a black hole, we got Apollo, a wonderfully waterful map filled with big baths of blue for players to swim in. This was the first time Battle Royale really saw a shake-up, so Apollo marked a big change in gameplay going forward.

ARTEMIS

Chapters: Chapter 2, Chapter 5: Season 5 (Chapter 2 Remix)
First Release: December 2021
Artemis is the underside of Apollo, revealed when The Seven flipped the island at the end of Chapter 2. This island features several landmarks and POIs from Apollo and Athena, and was the first island to feature collaboration locations (with The Daily Bugle).

ASTERIA

Chapters: Chapter 4
First Release: December 2022
When Artemis was destroyed by Chrome, its remains merged with Apollo and parts of other realities, creating Asteria. This was the first island to feature a Spawn Island in outer space, as well as the first to not feature any returning named locations.

HELIOS

Chapters: Chapter 5
First Release: December 2023
After naming islands after Greek Gods since day dot, Helios was the first island to actually feature Greek Gods, with its very own Mount Olympus. Helios was a map that was very international, with a train station featuring a number of different European languages.

ONINOSHIMA

Chapters: Chapter 6
First Release: December 2024
Oninoshima - Japanese for 'Island of Demons' - is the first island to have its name officially announced by Epic (yep, all previous islands were identified by the names found in their data files). This island takes inspiration from Japanese legends, and is split into distinct areas ruled by warring factions.

Oninoshima may seem like it's breaking with the Greek Mythology naming, but it's actually called 'Hermes' in the game's data files.

EMOTE QUIZ

Fortnite's emote collection has grown absolutely massive over the years, but here's the truth: some moves are just legendary while others... well, they exist. Think you can spot the most iconic celebration animations using just their tiny icons and a handful of letters as clues? Check out p. 62-63 for answers.

1

_E_ G_____

2

_A___I_ _P

3

C_____ A_____

4

B____ B_____

5
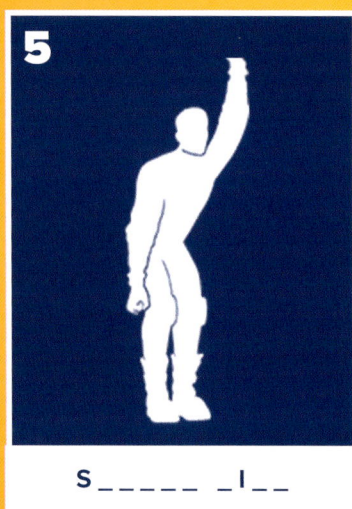
S_____ _I__

6

B_____ __W_

7

J_____ ___T____

8

T___ H_ _

9

F____

VICTORY ROYALE MAZE

Can you go from Battle Bus to Victory Royale without getting taken out by the other players, island wildlife or NPCs you run into along the way? Check out p. 62-63 for answers!

ISLAND WARS

The Fortnite islands have well and truly been through it. You probably think we're talking about the continuous drops of 99 bloodthirsty battlers getting dropped on it to fight to the death - sure, that can't be easy to play host to time and time again, but did you know that while that's happening, there's a whole other war for the island's very soul going on over in the narrative?

The game's storyline has been, to put it as politely as one possibly can, wilding since Day 1, but one thing has stayed consistent: there's always a good side, there's always a bad side, and they're always fighting over control of our dear, darling island. Some faces and factions come and go within a season or two, but here are some of the major players who have made their mark on the island.

THE GOOD GUYS

THE MIDAS CREW

Chapters Active:
Chapters 2-6
Key Members:
Midas, Brutus, Skye, Meowdas, Chaos Director, Jules, Meowscles, Deadpool, Agent Peely

First introduced as bad guys in Chapter 2's opening, this organisation of secret agents flipped the switch and have been protagonists ever since (with the odd dip back into villainy every now and then). Midas' Crew is made of three factions: GHOST, SHADOW, and those loyal only to Midas..

THE SEVEN

Chapters Active:
Chapters 1-3
Key Members:
The Foundation, The Origin, The Visitor, The Scientist, The Paradigm, The Imagined, The Order

The OG Good Guys (trademark pending), the Seven once stood to protect the Zero Point (the primordial heart of the Reality Zero), destroy the Loop and stop the Imagined Order. These mysterious members had no names, but were joined by familiar faces like Jonesy and the Avengers.

THE SUPERNOVAS

Chapters Active:
Chapter 6
Key Members: Hope, Jones, Superman, Peely, Fish Thicc, Haylee Skye, Morgan Myst, Ziggy, Synthwave, Killswitch, Lightrider

The evolution of the Demon Hunters, The Supernovas are a group of superheroes who fight under its leaders, Hope and Jonesy (with some help from Superman, of course). This team is funded by Midas, and were made to fight the threat of Daigo's Demon Warriors.

THE BAD GUYS

THE LAST REALITY

Chapters Active: Chapters 1-4
Key Members: The Nothing, The Cube Queen, The Herald, Storm Kings

Artemis is the underside of Apollo, revealed The Last Reality is an ancient, reality-crossing empire with one goal: to destroy all realities in the Omniverse. With armies beneath their banners, the Last Reality is led by The Nothing, a powerful cosmic entity that was the very first being in the Omniverse's existence. Their forces go beyond just armies; they are responsible for the island's shrinking Storms, and the Chrome that occasionally consumes them.

THE IMAGINED ORDER (IO)

Chapters Active: Chapters 2-3
Key Members: Geno, Doctor Slone, Agent Jones

The IO were introduced in Chapter 2, but were active for thousands of years before that. This multiversal organisation strived to create a 'perfect' civilization, travelling and manipulating realities to do so. They fought against the Seven after two of their members (and their leader's daughters) - The Imagined and The Order - defected and betrayed them to stop their evil plans.

THE DEMON WARRIORS

Chapters Active: Chapters 6
Key Members: Darkness, Daigo, Shogun X, Kor, The Night Rose

The Demon Warriors are an ancient threat to the island of Oninoshima; an army of demons (naturally) from the Spirit Realm that first arose after the Masks of Power were forged. Though once defeated, they were unleashed again upon Oninoshima when a Zero Point shard crashed onto the island.

SPOT THE DIFFERENCE

Can you spot the differences between these two pictures? There are eight differences in total. Check out p. 62-63 for answers.

FACTION SCRAMBLE

Fortnite's storyline has been absolutely wild, to put it mildly. Black holes swallowing entire realities, rifts tearing open new dimensions, timelines getting completely scrambled - the islands have truly seen it all. And who exactly is behind every world-ending event? Warring factions battling for ultimate control.

Think you've been keeping up with who's pulling the strings behind each chapter's madness? Time to put that lore knowledge to the test! We've mixed up the names of some major power players (though we left you the first letter as a hint) and paired them with their iconic logos. Can you crack the code and identify every faction?

1. TEH SVPUAERSNO

2. DENMO WIRRRSOA

3. TEH LTSA RLTAEYI

4. MISDA' CEWR

5. FXO CNAL

6. SOWAHD

7. TEH SNEEV

8. IDIMAEGN OEDRR

RED CARPET ROLL CALL

Fortnite has become a star-studded playground, packed with celebrity cameos. Can you recognize these iconic faces from their in-game looks? Check out p. 62-63 for answers.

1

2

3

4

5

6

7

8

9

10

11

12

TL;DR
SURVIVAL TIPS

Ready to claim that Victory Royale? Whether you're dropping hot for maximum chaos or playing it safe until the final showdown, nailing your 1v1 skills is absolutely crucial. The difference between heading back to the lobby and securing that crown often comes down to how well you handle those intense one-on-one moments.

SET UP YOUR SETUP

- Your game setup is basically your foundation - mess this up and you're fighting an uphill battle from the start. A universal tip is always to enable Turbo Build/Builder Pro (because nobody has time for slow construction when bullets are flying). From there, customise to best suit your personal playstyle.
- Keep your Autorun flexible setting flexible during a match. You'll want to flip it off during sneaky moments to avoid making unnecessary noise, then switch it back on for those cross-map rotations where you need your hands free to study the zone.
- Seriously, dive deep into those settings menus. Most players stick with defaults and miss out on tons of customization that could transform their entire experience. What works for streamers might not work for you, so experiment until everything feels natural.

Pro-tip! Between all the quest madness, NPCs, and whatever wild mechanics are active this season, the Storm becomes easy to ignore - until it melts you. Storm Sickness punishes zone-campers with triple damage, so respect those timers.

STORM EYE SHRINKS IN
1m 57s

AUDIO INTELLIGENCE

- Do yourself a massive favor and grab some headphones instead of relying on your speakers. Fortnite's audio design is incredibly detailed - those approaching footsteps and subtle environmental cues become crystal clear through proper headphones.
- Every gun makes different noises when players swap to them. Once you learn these patterns, you'll know if someone's about to spray you with an SMG or line up a sniper shot before they even peek.
- Plot twist: everyone else is listening too.
- Crouch-walk near combat zones because your footsteps are basically announcing your position to anyone paying attention.

KNOW WHEN TO HOLD BACK

- A healthy dose of paranoia has saved countless players from early eliminations. It's not playing scared; it's playing smart. When you spot premium loot just chilling in the open, assume it's a trap until proven otherwise. Someone's probably watching that exact spot with a rifle.

- After eliminating someone, fight the urge to immediately give in to loot-blindness and channel your focus into working out which plundered pieces are worth picking up. Your battle probably sent up flares to every nearby player, so secure the area first (and if you're in the late game, consider throwing up some quick walls before you sort through your spoils).

YOU WERE NEVER EVEN HERE...

- Aggression feels great, but survival requires brain over brawn. Skip the obvious stuff like bush-camping and focus on smart details: don't completely destroy trees (that falling animation is like a beacon), and always reset doors after looting (open doors = "someone was definitely here").

- Treat open areas like lava - only cross them when you have zero other options. Someone's always watching from high ground, and cover gives you time to think instead of just panic-building when shots start flying.

- Also, be mindful of your builds. Spamming ramps and walls might save you in a fight, but it also leaves behind a massive "Hey! I was here :)". Build only when you need to, and don't hesitate to destroy behind you either.

WHAT'S YOUR PLAYSTYLE?

At the end of the day, Fortnite's a wild mix of skill and luck. You might have the cleanest aim in the lobby, but that won't stop a random wolf from catching you a corner on your last bandies, or someone landing a millisecond faster and grabbing the shotgun you were going for. Every match is a fresh roll of the dice - the island's unpredictable, the loot spawns are random, and chaos is pretty much guaranteed. But there's one thing you can control: how you play. Whether you're all about pushing fights or hanging back to plan your next move, your playstyle is what shapes every game.

THE CLASSIC

Classic players are the ultimate all-rounders who refuse to pick favourites when the game serves up so many delicious options. Why limit yourself to just one trick when Fortnite's got a whole buffet of mechanics to feast on? These legends embrace the full package: tweaking their gear setup, wandering around for loot, throwing up walls when things get spicy, and engaging in a lil' scrap when the mood strikes.

This approach is perfect for rookies who want to taste everything Fortnite has to offer and figure out their vibe, but don't be mistaken - this doesn't have to be a phase. Even vets gravitate toward this style when they want to kick back and enjoy the ride without the pressure.

THE ARCHITECT

Building is what separates Fortnite from every other battle royale out there, and Architects live for those construction moments. Sure, they can handle their weapons just fine, but hand them some mats and watch them become absolute wizards. They control the flow of a fight because they can totally reshape the battlefield - launching battles into the clouds or trapping opponents in wooden coffins. RIP, either way.

This style demands serious dedication and lightning reflexes that only come from grinding and developing muscle-memory fast building inputs. Real Architects spend their downtime in Creative mode, perfecting their craft so they can unleash architectural chaos when it counts.

THE HITMAN

These players don't mess around - they're here for one thing and one thing only: racking up eliminations. Hitmen load up on serious firepower so they've got the perfect tool for every takedown scenario. Forget fishing trips; these warriors live for bounty hunts and those sweet, sweet elimination rewards.

This isn't a beginner-friendly path - it's built for players who've already cut their teeth on shooters and know how to aim under pressure. The skill ceiling is sky-high, demanding tons of practice and razor-sharp reflexes to pull off those clutch plays consistently.

THE NINJA

Ninjas are the ghosts of the battlefield; you won't spot them coming until you're on your back and your loot is spilled on the ground around you, and you might not even show face then, either. They're just as elimination-focused as Hitmen, but you'll never catch them going in guns blazing. These shadow warriors are all about the art of the sneak attack, turning every encounter into a deadly game of cat and mouse.

This style clicks with players who prefer picking off targets from a distance rather than getting up close and personal. Ninjas also love the game's sneakier tools: setting clever traps and using disguises that leave other players scratching their heads wondering what just happened.

PEACEKEEPERS

Like Ninjas, Peacekeepers master the art of staying invisible, but they're not hunting for their next victim. Sometimes the best strategy is simply outlasting everyone else - dodging the storm, avoiding angry NPCs, and exploring every corner of the map for as long as possible. You'd be amazed how often playing it safe can land you in the final circles without firing a single shot.

This playstyle is ideal for anyone who wants to soak up all the island's secrets and experiment with the latest features the devs keep dropping. It's also clutch for players grinding through challenges and trying to complete their collection goals.

PICK YOUR PLAYSTYLE

Not sure which of the five playstyles suit you best? Answer these questions below to find out!

1. You land at a hot drop location with tons of other players. What's your first move?

- [ ] A. Grab the nearest weapon and start looking for fights.
- [ ] B. Find a quiet spot to loot up, then decide what to do based on what gear you find.
- [ ] C. Quickly gather mats and start building protective walls while you loot.
- [ ] D. Sneak around the edges, staying hidden while other players fight each other.
- [ ] E. Avoid the chaos entirely and rotate to a safer area to loot in peace.

2. You spot an enemy player in the distance. What's your play?

- [ ] A. Rush them head-on with your best weapon and engage in direct combat.
- [ ] B. Assess the situation first - check your loadout, their position, and plan accordingly.
- [ ] C. Build up for high ground advantage before engaging.
- [ ] D. Try to get closer without being seen and eliminate them with a surprise attack.
- [ ] E. Keep your distance and avoid the confrontation unless absolutely necessary.

3. You're in the final circles with a stellar loadout. What's your strategy?

- [ ] A. Go aggressive to get your kill count as high as possible before the match ends.
- [ ] B. Play it by ear - adapt to whatever situation develops with the remaining players.
- [ ] C. Build a fortress and control the high ground for the final showdown.
- [ ] D. Stay hidden and let other players fight each other, then strike when they're weak.
- [ ] E. Find the best hiding spot and wait for the storm to force the final confrontation.

4. A new season just dropped with fresh mechanics and items. What excites you most?

- [ ] A. New weapons to master and AI to eliminate with them.
- [ ] B. Trying out all the new features.
- [ ] C. Map updates means new features to integrate into builds.
- [ ] D. Sneaky new items like disguises or traps to use for surprise attacks.
- [ ] E. New areas to explore and secrets to discover across the updated map.

5. You're low on health with limited healing items. What do you do?

- [ ] A. Push forward anyway - sometimes the best defense is a good offense.
- [ ] B. Weigh your options and make the smartest play based on your current situation.
- [ ] C. Build defensive structures to protect yourself while you heal up safely.
- [ ] D. Find a hiding spot where you can heal without being detected.
- [ ] E. Rotate to a quieter area of the map to avoid fights until you're back to full health.

6. Your squad wants to take on a boss fight. How do you contribute?

- ☐ A. Lead the charge with heavy firepower and take point on the assault.
- ☐ B. Fill whatever role the team needs - support, damage, or crowd control.
- ☐ C. Build structures to protect the team and control the battlefield.
- ☐ D. Flank around and attack from unexpected angles while the boss focuses on your team.
- ☐ E. Provide intel about the area and watch for third parties trying to crash the fight.

7. You find a Legendary weapon but your inventory is full. What gets dropped?

- ☐ A. Whatever weapon has the lowest damage output - you need max firepower.
- ☐ B. Depends on the weapon type and what situations you expect to face.
- ☐ C. Probably healing items since you can always build cover to protect yourself.
- ☐ D. Utility items that might give away your position or make noise.
- ☐ E. Combat items you're least comfortable with - stick to what you know works.

8. The storm is closing and you need to rotate. How do you move?

- ☐ A. Take the most direct route and fight anyone who gets in your way.
- ☐ B. Check the map and choose the route that gives you the best options.
- ☐ C. Build your way across dangerous areas to maintain safety and high ground.
- ☐ D. Use natural cover and stay out of sight while moving to the safe zone.
- ☐ E. Take the longest route if it means avoiding other players entirely.

Mostly A's - The Hitman

You're all about the action! You live for eliminations and direct confrontation. Your aggressive playstyle keeps matches exciting and your aim skills sharp.

Mostly B's - The Classic

You're the ultimate all-rounder who adapts to any situation. You enjoy every aspect of Fortnite and make decisions based on what the moment demands.

Mostly C's - The Architect

Building is your superpower! You control fights by reshaping the battlefield and turning raw materials into victory through superior construction skills.

Mostly D's - The Ninja

You're the master of stealth and surprise. You prefer calculated strikes over direct confrontation, using cunning and patience to outplay opponents.

Mostly E's - The Peacekeeper

You're the strategic survivor who wins through patience and positioning. You'd rather outlast opponents than outgun them, exploring and surviving your way to victory.

KEEPING UP WITH JONESY

He's been a soldier, a scientist, a secret agent, and even a smoothie (versatile King). His style is unmatched: from camo and flip-flops, to tuxedos and tank tops. Whether you call him Jonesy, Agent Jones, John Jones, or that blonde dude from the lobby, one thing's for sure: he's Fortnite's most iconic face.

First showing up all the way back in Chapter 1, Season 1, Jonesy started as a basic default skin, but don't let that simple look fool you. Over time, Jonesy became one of the most important characters in Fortnite's ever-evolving story - and the game wouldn't be the same without him.

BEING JOHN JONES

At this point, Fortnite has had many Chapters, many seasons, and many realities - that means we've gotten a lot of Jonesies over the years.

There's no official count, but between Battle Pass skins, NPC versions, and Item Shop styles, there are dozens of Jonesy variants. Some are goofy. Some are gritty. Some are just... covered in fish. Here are a few of his most iconic forms:

- **Jonesy The First:** AKA OG Jonesy - as a Default skin, Jonesy looked every inch the rugged adventurer. Blond, sleeveless, inexplicable scarf - he had it all.
- **Agent Jones:** The moment everything changed. This version of Jonesy went rogue from the Imagined Order, ripped his sleeves off, and dove straight into the multiverse.
- **Bunker Jonesy:** It's giving Tom Hanks in Castaway (a throwback reference for sure, but those who know, know) - long beard, long hair, and lots of conspiracy theories. He'd been surviving underground solo, and may or may not have gone a little bonkers.
- **Scuba Jonesy:** A rare chill moment for Jonesy, this version is decked out in scuba gear and ready for a vacation (and always ready for a surprise ambush).
- **Unchained Jonesy:** Breaking free from the IO's prison, this Jonesy is bruised, battered, and officially done following orders.
- **Slurp Jonesy:** Half-man, half-Slurp Juice. Most definitely sticky.

Bunker Jonesy may have looked crazy, but he could predict the future. The scribblings on his hideout wall seemed to foretell future game events, like the Cube and Mecha Team Leader.

STORYLINE SUPERSTAR

Jonesy isn't just Fortnite's poster boy, he's deep in the lore. From mysterious agent to multiverse rebel, he's been at the center of some of Fortnite's biggest moments, and is quite literally the familiar thread for players to cling to through the wild ride of Fortnite's storyline.

- **Chapter 2: The Device (Season 2)** Jonesy emerges from the shadows as Agent Jones of the Imagined Order (IO), orchestrating reality-bending events behind the scenes.
- **Chapter 2: Zero Crisis Finale (Season 6)** He betrays the IO and teams up with The Foundation to stabilize the chaotic Zero Point. This pivotal moment transforms him from obedient agent to island savior.
- **Chapter 3: Flipside & Resistance (Seasons 1-2)** With the island flipped and war raging between IO and The Seven, Jones fully commits to the rebellion, leading resistance forces against his former employers.
- **Chapter 3: Collision Event** Jones and The Foundation pilot the massive Mecha Strike Commander in an epic showdown, then venture beneath the island to end the IO threat permanently.
- **Chapter 4: Post-IO Era** Jones steps back as new villains emerge. With IO defeated, he makes occasional appearances while fresh factions like The Oathbound and Reality Augments reshape the island.
- **Chapter 5: Underground Agent** Jones resurfaces with The Underground, a resistance group battling the shadowy Society that now controls the island. He's battle-hardened, experienced, and sporting yet another fresh look.
- **Chapter 6: Galactic Guardian** Vengeance Jones pops up at Supernova Academy, where he guides players against demonic forces and cosmic invaders threatening the island.

SHIELD SPLASH PUZZLE

Time to heal up - and you're the designated Squad Medic. Can you work out which Shield Potion the Shield Keg will fill first? Check out p. 62-63 for answers.

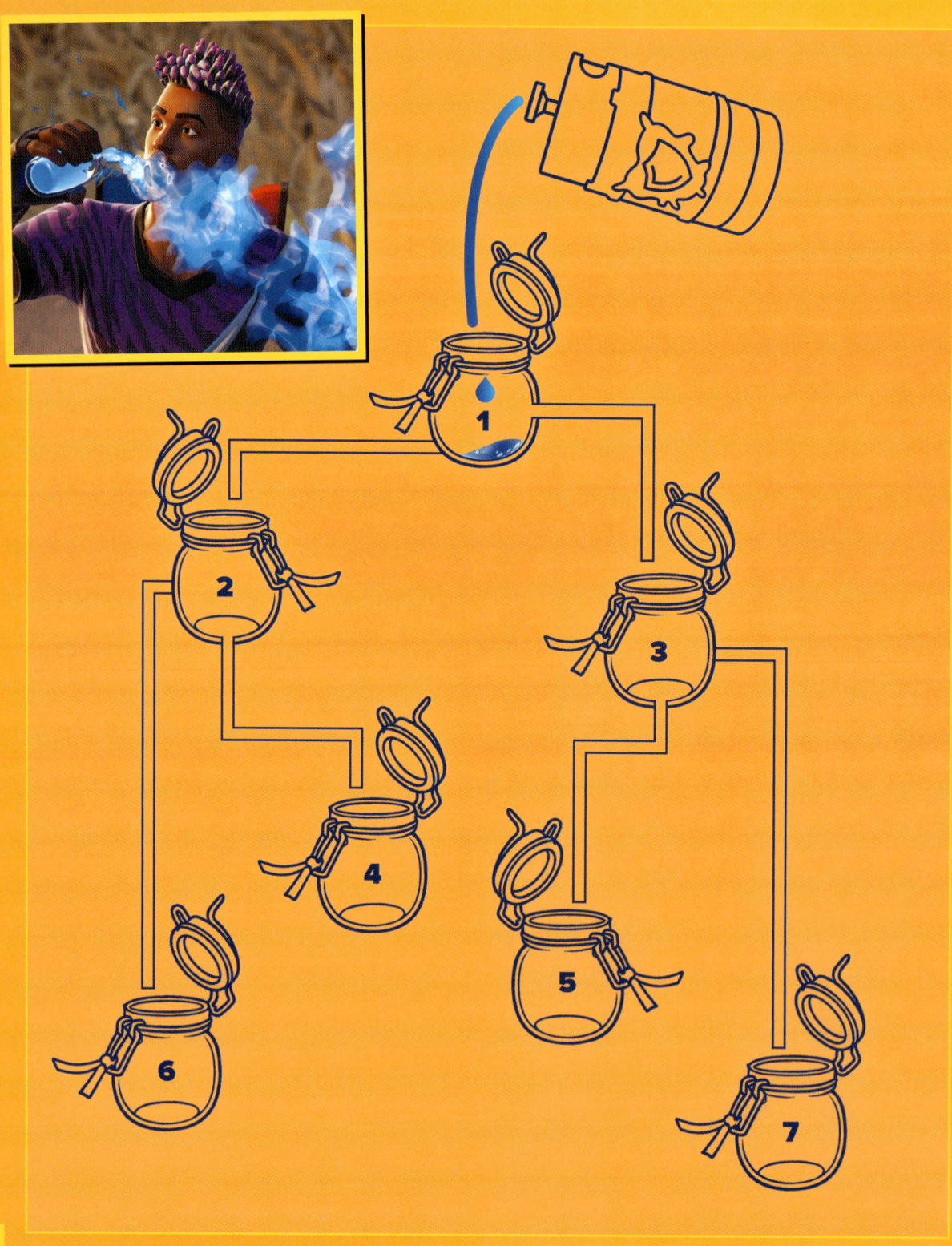

LLAMA RUN

A loot llama has dropped from the skies! Can you work out who's going to make it to the fabled haul first? Check out p. 62-63 for answers.

A

B

C

FORTNITE FACTS

Think you know everything about Fortnite? Think again! From unbelievable player stats to unexpected crossovers, here's a bunch of facts that prove Fortnite is still the biggest name in gaming.

FORTNITE FOREVER

Over 650 million people have registered Fortnite accounts as of 2025. That's more than double the population of the United States! Safe to say, the Battle Bus is getting a little crowded.

Oh, and that 650 million is a **30% jump** since 2022, meaning the game has added more than 150 million players in just three years.

Fortnite racks up more than **110 million monthly active players,** with over 60 million showing up daily. For perspective, that's the equivalent of the entire population of Italy jumping from the Battle Bus every single day.

On its busiest day ever, **44.7 million players** logged in within 24 hours. What was the occasion? The Fortnite OG event. Numerical proof that nothing hits harder than nostalgia.

Fortnite's global dominance shows no sign of slowing: its lifetime revenue has **surpassed $40 billion.** That beats the combined global box office of every Marvel film ever released.

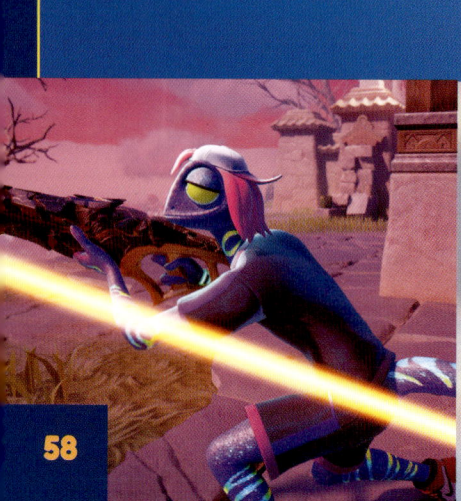

COMMUNITY WINS

User-generated islands now account for a whopping **36.5% of all Fortnite playtime.** That's 5.23 billion hours spent in community creations in one year.

And that 36.5% is up **5% from 2023** - meaning over a third of Fortnite sessions now take place inside player-built worlds.

Since Epic rolled out Unreal Editor for Fortnite (UEFN), the community has exploded, which led to nearly **200,000 new islands** being published in a single year.

Fortnite has paid out a staggering **$352 million to Creative and UEFN creators in 2024.** Seven of those creators earned more than $10 million each, while a total of 58 made over $1 million.

Top-tier creators earn serious cash: in 2024, nine developers took home 40 % of the total payout, and one **top earner made over $20 million.** That puts Fortnite's creator economy in the same income ballpark as Hollywood screenwriters.

HUH... THAT'S RANDOM

In Chapter 6 Season 3, Epic hid what players now call the Briefcase of Patience near Volpine Fall. It gives epic loot - but only if you hold the open button for a full ten minutes, becoming a total sitting duck. It's trolling with loot built in.

Back in Season 1, players discovered that editing brick walls gave a super slim chance of spawning a little garden gnome tucked between the bricks. Rumour says it can still be found in current versions - rarer than a unicorn, but priceless when you spot it.

The lovable Mancake skin wears a pad of butter on his head that actually melts away during a match, dripping until it disappears. It's one of those moments you see Epic's attention to detail that makes you stop mid-battle and chuckle.

HOW LONG WILL YOU SURVIVE?

Ready to test your knowledge and see just how long you'd last on the island? This quiz dives into all the key gameplay moves: from smart looting and building to tricky fights and storm survival. Answer the questions and find out if you've got what it takes to dodge danger, outplay opponents, and clutch that Victory Royale. Check out p. 62-63 for answers and see how long you'd survive down there.

1. What's the smartest move to make in the first 30 seconds after you land?
- A. Run to the nearest road and look for a vehicle
- B. Search nearby chests and grab a weapon
- C. Swing your pickaxe at random objects

2. Which of these is the highest weapon rarity?
- A. Legendary
- B. Rare (Blue)
- C. Epic (Purple)

3. What's the max number of materials (wood, brick, metal) you can carry per type?
- A. 500
- B. 999
- C. Unlimited

4. What does building primarily help with in Fortnite?
- A. Blocking storm damage
- B. Gaining high ground and protection
- C. Finding hidden chests

5. Which item restores both health and shields over time?
- A. Big Shield Potion
- B. Small Shield Potion
- C. Slurp Juice

6. Which of these is a good strategy for spotting enemies?
- A. Walking along roads
- B. Staying on high ground
- C. Swimming in rivers

7. What is the best close-range weapon type?
- A. Shotgun
- B. Assault Rifle
- C. Crossbow

8. You're far from the safe zone and the storm is closing in. What should you do?
- A. Build a tower and scout
- B. Start rotating early to avoid panic fights
- C. Camp in place and wait for other players to pass

9. What's the purpose of a Reboot Van?
- A. Spawns loot
- B. Heals you
- C. Reboots teammates

10. After a tough 1v1, you barely survive with 20 HP. What should you do?

- A. Grab your opponent's loot
- B. Heal up and reload all your weapons
- C. Run toward the center of the circle

11. What's a "third party" in Fortnite terms?

- A. Watching someone else's fight
- B. Crashing a fight between two other players
- C. Making a squad of three

12. You hear footsteps above you but don't have visual yet. What's the safest play?

- A. Build up and rush them immediately
- B. Emote to throw them off
- C. Crouch, stay hidden, and wait for an opening

13. Why is crouching useful when sneaking?

- A. It makes your footsteps quieter
- B. It helps avoid fall damage
- C. It increases your damage

14. Which item gives the most health at once?

- A. Bandages
- B. Big Shield Potion
- C. Medkit

15. Why should you aim for the blue circle when using your pickaxe?

- A. It breaks the object faster
- B. It makes less noise
- C. It gives you extra Gold

16. Which of these is best for long-range attacks?

- A. SMG
- B. Shotgun
- C. Sniper Rifle

17. What's the main risk of looting in the open?

- A. Getting stuck in a tree
- B. Being spotted and shot
- C. Running out of building mats

18. Why do players rotate early during storm circles?

- A. To get more kills
- B. To avoid fighting while moving
- C. To build giant towers

19. When pushing an enemy player, what's the smartest way to start the fight?

- A. Run straight at them with your shotgun out
- B. Shoot from far away to warn them
- C. Take high ground and tag them with ranged fire first

20. Which of these is a smart loadout combo?

- A. Shotgun + Sniper + Heals
- B. Two SMGs + Heals
- C. Sniper + Sniper + Sniper

SO HOW LONG DID YOU SURVIVE?

0-5 CORRECT
Storm Victim:
Yikes! You didn't even make it past the first zone. Time to hit the Battle Lab and train up.

6-10 CORRECT
Midgame Mayhem:
You've got some potential, but those rotations and loadouts need work. Watch your back and your storm timer!

11-15 CORRECT
Top Ten Threat:
Not bad! You're building, healing, and choosing fights like a pro. Just polish up your endgame decisions.

16-19 CORRECT
Final Circle Survivor:
You're storm smart, loot wise, and ready for sweaty lobbies. One clutch away from a crown.

20/20 CORRECT
Victory Royale Master:
You're a Fortnite genius! Walls, weapons, and wins - you've got it all. Wear that crown with pride.

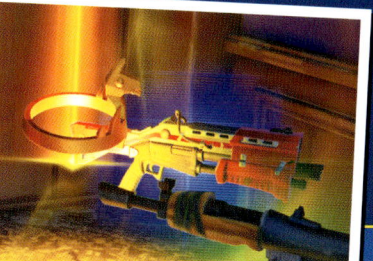

ANSWERS

26 Character Crossword

Across:
3. NISHA
4. JOHNJONES
8. DOCTORSLONE
9. MIDAS
10. THE FOUNDATION
12. PEELY

Down:
1. HAYLESKYE
2. BANDLETT
5. DAIGO
6. MEWSCLES
7. CAAMITH
11. FISHSTICK

27 Spot the Difference

36 Crosshair Match-Up

37 Weapon Wordsearch

C	B	X	G	S	I	X	S	H	O	O	T	E	R	N	N	Y	K	S	S
S	A	V	A	T	K	O	W	A	Y	R	W	X	S	C	P	X	D	H	T
C	S	A	T	D	H	X	B	Z	O	D	N	H	P	C	P	W	Q	C	O
W	S	W	E	V	G	E	S	Z	R	L	N	B	D	N	U	S	P	S	R
E	B	U	K	C	F	F	D	U	E	L	F	I	R	E	R	I	P	S	M
D	O	Y	E	L	X	J	M	U	N	A	W	E	G	E	M	D	R	S	S
A	O	E	E	I	D	G	M	Q	B	X	H	O	G	H	M	K	Z	I	C
N	S	O	P	Z	U	P	N	G	T	C	E	N	B	P	T	F	F	W	O
E	T	W	E	N	S	N	B	S	N	P	F	W	G	L	B	P	E	U	
R	Q	W	R	B	A	I	V	U	O	L	Y	G	C	P	A	Z	A	H	T
G	P	U	P	C	G	A	A	R	C	J	J	Y	R	G	V	A	M	K	W	I
S	N	P	D	C	D	L	O	Y	D	D	N	K	K	Z	S	I	P	P	K
P	H	N	H	D	T	N	U	G	I	N	I	M	O	A	D	Q	N	R	O
C	A	I	W	E	C	O	M	B	A	T	S	H	O	T	G	U	N	G	P
H	L	K	K	B	O	O	G	I	E	B	O	M	B	Q	Y	V	M	D	L
L	F	C	E	D	A	L	B	Y	T	I	N	I	F	N	I	B	J	R	O
X	O	T	R	W	S	A	V	C	Z	E	X	W	Z	W	T	D	Y	L	T
R	X	J	F	R	G	Y	T	M	R	Q	G	C	F	G	D	O	X	S	
M	R	N	E	K	D	S	Y	C	N	W	T	E	X	A	C	I	W	X	I
Z	E	X	I	T	W	M	Y	A	V	O	R	Y	O	P	R	V	I	J	P

40 Emote Quiz

1. GET GRIDDY
2. LAUGH IT UP
3. CROWNING ACHIEVEMENT
4. BILLY BOUNCE
5. SURFIN BIRD
6. BOOGIE DOWN
7. JABBA SWITCHWAY
8. TAKE THE L
9. FRESH